How To Play
GREAT BLUES RIFFS
VOLUME 1
By Michael P. Wolfsohn

Riffs in All Styles from Traditional Blues to Contemporary Rock
CHERRY LANE RIFFS SERIES

Edited by Jon Chappell
Music Engraving by W.R. Music Service
Production Manager: Daniel Rosenbaum
Art Direction: Alisa Hill
Administration: Marianne Monroe
Director of Music: Mark Phillips

Photography by Peter Amft

*Photos of Michael Wolfsohn and hand positions
by Robert Ellis*

ISBN: 0-89524-508-6

CONTENTS

5

How To Use This Book

6

Chapter I: Blues Progressions

11

Chapter II: The Blues Scale

19

Chapter III: Riffs and How To Use Them

ACKNOWLEDGEMENTS

Thanks to:

Jon Chappell and everyone at Cherry Lane Music for making this book possible.

Danny Kalb and Mike Bloomfield for those first recordings that got me into the blues.

Bruce Iglauer at Alligator Records & Artist Management for keeping the blues on record and supplying a lot of the recordings that I drew on for this book.

Roger Sadowsky for making a guitar that *sings.*

My wife, Jayne, for patience beyond patience while I disappeared under the headphones (again).

And last, all of the great musicians who have made — and keep making — all of that great blues music.

M.W.

TABLATURE EXPLANATION

TABLATURE: A six-line staff that graphically represents the guitar fingerboard. By placing a number on the appropriate line, the string and fret of any note can be indicated. For example:

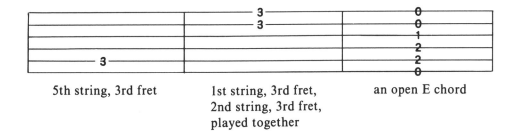

5th string, 3rd fret   1st string, 3rd fret, 2nd string, 3rd fret, played together   an open E chord

Definitions for Special Guitar Notation (For both traditional and tablature guitar lines)

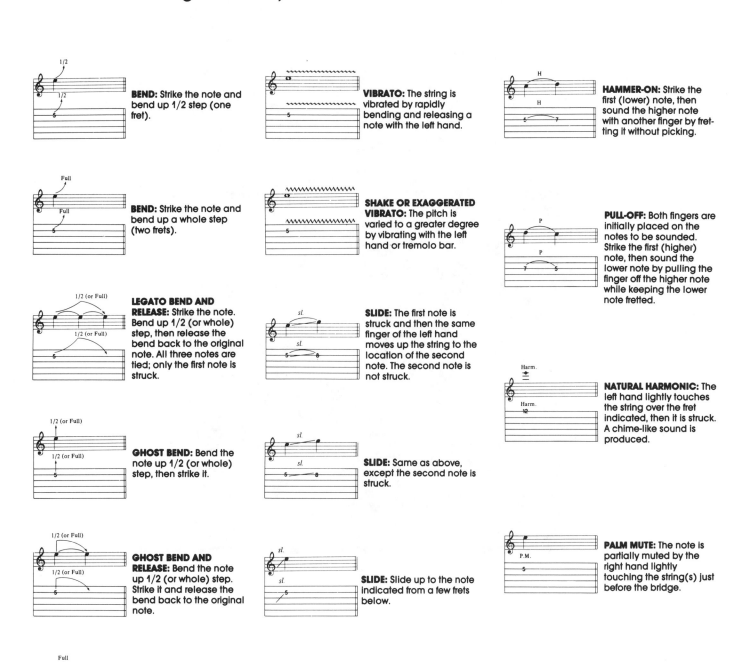

BEND: Strike the note and bend up 1/2 step (one fret).

BEND: Strike the note and bend up a whole step (two frets).

LEGATO BEND AND RELEASE: Strike the note. Bend up 1/2 (or whole) step, then release the bend back to the original note. All three notes are tied; only the first note is struck.

GHOST BEND: Bend the note up 1/2 (or whole) step, then strike it.

GHOST BEND AND RELEASE: Bend the note up 1/2 (or whole) step. Strike it and release the bend back to the original note.

UNISON BEND: The lower note is struck slightly before the higher. It is then bent to the pitch of the higher note. They are on adjacent strings.

VIBRATO: The string is vibrated by rapidly bending and releasing a note with the left hand.

SHAKE OR EXAGGERATED VIBRATO: The pitch is varied to a greater degree by vibrating with the left hand or tremolo bar.

SLIDE: The first note is struck and then the same finger of the left hand moves up the string to the location of the second note. The second note is not struck.

SLIDE: Same as above, except the second note is struck.

SLIDE: Slide up to the note indicated from a few frets below.

SLIDE: Strike the note and slide up an indefinite number of frets, releasing finger pressure at the end of the slide.

HAMMER-ON: Strike the first (lower) note, then sound the higher note with another finger by fretting it without picking.

PULL-OFF: Both fingers are initially placed on the notes to be sounded. Strike the first (higher) note, then sound the lower note by pulling the finger off the higher note while keeping the lower note fretted.

NATURAL HARMONIC: The left hand lightly touches the string over the fret indicated, then it is struck. A chime-like sound is produced.

PALM MUTE: The note is partially muted by the right hand lightly touching the string(s) just before the bridge.

MUFFLED STRINGS: A percussive sound is produced by laying the left hand across the strings without depressing them to the fretboard and striking them with the right hand.

Little Milton

How To Use This Book

Learning how to play the blues is one of the best ways to get started at improvising rock guitar. This book is designed to show you how to play both lead and rhythm styles, and you will also learn many of the riffs of the blues greats.

To use this book, all you need is to be able to use a pick, play well enough that you can form a barre A chord at the fifth fret, and read chord diagrams. Everything else is in this book.

People learn best at different rates, and in different ways. In order to make this book as useable as possible for as many people as possible, I have marked several types of material in distinctive ways.

The Basics

Material under this heading is essential. This is the minimum you need to know to be able to work with the current section of the book.

Technical Tips

Material under this heading is about technique—physical control of your guitar. It will usually discuss a method which makes it easier to perform something described in the chapter.

Theory Notes

Material under this heading is about the theory (note and chord relationships, etc.) that you are working with in the current section.

If you already know how to play the chords and patterns taught in Chapter I, review them and go on. If you already know all the positions of the blues scale taught in Chapter II, review them and go on. If you are just interested in the riffs and ways of using them, go right to Chapter III.

Remember, patience and practice are both necessary to play well. The more time you can devote to playing, the sooner you will master your instrument. Also, regularity is important; a small amount of daily work is much better than large blocks of time every few days.

Learning rarely happens smoothly. It is much more likely that you will have quick bursts of new ability followed by a longer period when you won't seem to be improving much. Actually, what's happening at this time is that you are assimilating what you have learned, and getting ready for the next burst. Try to be patient during these slow times.

Now, let's play the blues!

—Michael P. Wolfsohn

Chapter I. Blues Progressions

Most blues progressions are made up of three chords (there are some exceptions). These chords are in a relationship known as I-IV-V. We will start by learning these chords for the key of A.

The Basics

You'll need to know how to play an A7 barre chord at the fifth fret, a D9 chord at the fourth fret and an E9 chord at the sixth fret.

Here are diagrams for these three chords:

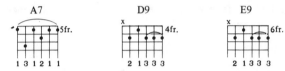

You'll need to be able to hyperextend (bend backwards) the first joint of your ring finger to play the 9th-chords.

This is how a bar of a rhythm guitar part will be notated:

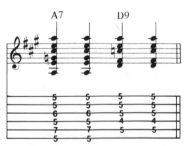

The large vertical rules indicate measure or bar lines. These divide the music into rhythmic sections. The slashes represent the counts within the measure. In this example, there are four counts in the measure (shown by the numbers beneath the bar). The chord symbols (A7, D9) show what chord or chords are to be played during the measure. In this example, they are placed over the first and third slashes, telling you to play an A7 chord beginning on the first beat of the measure, and a D9 chord beginning on the third beat of the measure.

This type of notation tells you only where the chord changes are, not what to play. You can play many different rhythm guitar styles with any of these chord progressions. Different rhythm styles will be explained in the text and illustrated in the music and tablature.

Here is the same bar of rhythm guitar in standard music notation and tablature, so that you may compare them.

Listen to Ex. 1 on your tape. This is a *swing* or *sock* rhythm. In this example, the guitar is playing one full down-stroke (all six strings in the A7 chord, all five strings in the D9 and E9 chords) on each beat. Beats 2 and 4 are accented (played slightly louder) and the chord is briefly muted after beats 2 and 4. This helps to define the rhythm, and push the tune along. Here's one bar of this pattern in music and tab:

This is a standard 12-bar blues progression. There are several ways you can play this.

A7
| ╱ ╱ ╱ ╱ | ╱ ╱ ╱ ╱ | ╱ ╱ ╱ ╱ | ╱ ╱ ╱ ╱ |

D9   A7
| ╱ ╱ ╱ ╱ | ╱ ╱ ╱ ╱ | ╱ ╱ ╱ ╱ | ╱ ╱ ╱ ╱ |

E9   D9   A7   E9
| ╱ ╱ ╱ ╱ | ╱ ╱ ╱ ╱ | ╱ ╱ ╱ ╱ | ╱ ╱ ╱ ╱ ‖

Listen to Ex. 2 on your tape. This is a slow shuffle rhythm. The guitar in this example is playing a triplet pattern—that is, the guitar plays three strokes per beat. On beat 1, play all six strings with the first stroke, and strings 1, 2 and 3 for the next two strokes. On beat 2, play strings 1, 2 and 3 for all three strokes. Repeat this pattern for beats 3 and 4. Accent the first stroke of beats 2 and 4. This pattern is played with downstrokes only.

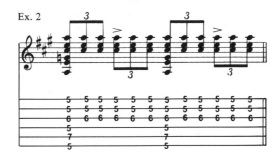

Listen to Ex. 3 on your tape. This is a muted shuffle rhythm. Play twice the open 5th string with the 4th string fretted at the 2nd fret. Then play twice the open 5th string with the 4th string fretted at the 4th fret. This produces the familiar boogie-woogie sound. This pattern replaces the A7 chord in the chord progression.

For all shuffle-type progressions used in this book, the rhythm ♩ ♪ (♩♩♩) will be abbreviated as swing eighths (♩ ♩).

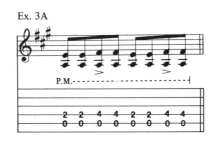

In this example, the strings of the guitar are slightly muted by placing the side of the right hand exactly on the bridge. Precise placement is important to get this sound. If you are too far behind the bridge, no muting will occur. If you are too far in front of the bridge, you will be over-muting, and will hear only clicks. Here's how your hand should look:

Moving this pattern over to strings 4 & 3 gives you the pattern to replace the D9 chord in our progression.

Moving the pattern to strings 6 & 5 gives you the substitute pattern for E9.

Notice, once again, that each beat is divided into three parts. You play only on the first and third parts of each beat (the second part is silent).

Try playing all of these along with your tape. Ex. 4 on your tape is the complete, standard 12-bar blues. The guitar is on the right channel, and the rest of the band is on the left. First, practice matching the recorded guitar, then practice playing along with the band with the recorded guitar turned off.

Here are two more common blues progressions. You can play any of the rhythm styles you have learned with them. These appear as Ex. 5 and Ex. 6 on your tape. Once again, the guitar is recorded on the right channel, and the rest of the band is recorded on the left.

Ex. 5

| A7 | | D9 | | A7 | | | |
| / / / / | / / / / | / / / / | / / / / |

| D9 | | | A7 | | | |
| / / / / | / / / / | / / / / | / / / / |

| E9 | | D9 | | A7 | | E9 | |
| / / / / | / / / / | / / / / | / / / / |

Ex. 6

```
D9                          A7
| ∕  ∕  ∕  ∕ | ∕  ∕  ∕  ∕ | ∕  ∕  ∕  ∕ | ∕  ∕  ∕  ∕ |

D9                          A7
| ∕  ∕  ∕  ∕ | ∕  ∕  ∕  ∕ | ∕  ∕  ∕  ∕ | ∕  ∕  ∕  ∕ |

E9            D9            A7            E9
| ∕  ∕  ∕  ∕ | ∕  ∕  ∕  ∕ | ∕  ∕  ∕  ∕ | ∕  ∕  ∕  ∕ ‖
```

Some blues progressions contain both riffs and chords. Here is an example of a riff that can be used in a progression. This appears as Ex. 7A on your tape.

Ex. 7A

This particular riff takes up two bars. Other riffs that you might use this way could be longer or shorter.

Now, here is an entire progression combining riffs and chords. This is Ex. 7B on the tape.

The riff is played twice as an intro and twice before each new verse, making this a14-bar progression.

Ex. 7B

```
N.C.
| ∕  ∕  ∕  ∕ | ∕  ∕  ∕  ∕ | ∕  ∕  ∕  ∕ | ∕  ∕  ∕  ∕ ‖
Riff                       Riff

   D9                          A7
‖: ∕  ∕  ∕  ∕ | ∕  ∕  ∕  ∕ | ∕  ∕  ∕  ∕ | ∕  ∕  ∕  ∕ |
                            Riff

D9                          A7
| ∕  ∕  ∕  ∕ | ∕  ∕  ∕  ∕ | ∕  ∕  ∕  ∕ | ∕  ∕  ∕  ∕ |
                            Riff

E9         D9         A7
| ∕ ∕ ∕ ∕ | ∕ ∕ ∕ ∕ | ∕ ∕ ∕ ∕ | ∕ ∕ ∕ ∕ | ∕ ∕ ∕ ∕ | ∕ ∕ ∕ ∕ :‖
                Riff              Riff
```

Technical Tips

Using a stiffer pick, and learning to hold it loosely will help make your playing smoother and more controlled. The pick should be held so that the point comes straight out of the side of your thumb, and plays exactly flat against the string. A sharper point will give you a brighter sound than a round point.

Working with your tape both with and without the recorded guitar will help you get a feel for the styles you are learning, and will help you develop steady timing. The ability to play in steady time is one of the most important skills a rhythm guitarist can develop. It enables you to lock in with a bass player and drummer to create a tight groove, or to provide a steady rhythm for another guitarist to jam against if there's just two of you.

Once you have your rhythm steady, you're ready to start learning lead. Then, you and other musicians can take turns playing lead and rhythm, giving everyone an opportunity to express himself. In the next chapter, we will begin to explore the tools of the lead guitarist, and how they are used to build great riffs and solos.

Theory Notes

You have been playing A7, D9 and E9 chords. The 9th-chords are actually substitutes for D7 and E7. One of the unique things about blues progressions is that all of the chords used are 7ths or substitutes for 7ths. If you know or can learn some of these substitute chords, you can add a lot of color to your rhythm playing. The most common substitutes for 7ths are 9ths, 11ths and 13ths. Below are diagrams for one form of the E11 and one form of the A13. Try these out and see how the sound of your progression changes. You can also raise or lower the 5th or 9th of 7th chords to get a different color, as in this form of a D7#9.

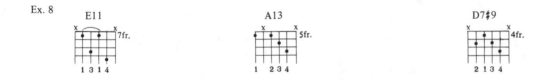

Chapter II. The Blues Scale

Most blues and rock lead guitar is based on the blues scale. In this chapter, we will learn what this scale is, and how to play parts of it in six positions (3rd position, 5th position, 8th position,10th position,12th position and 15th position). A *position* on the guitar is a group of four consecutive frets (one for each finger) and is named for the lowest numbered fret (the one you play with your first finger).

The Basics

You must be able to play a scale from a neck diagram, such as the one below.

Ex. 9

This is a diagram of an A minor pentatonic scale. Basically, it is a picture of a portion of the neck of your guitar as you look down at it. The numbers indicate the strings. (Remember, string 1 is your high E, string 6 is your low E.) The dots indicate which strings and frets to play, and the position dictates which fingers are used. In fifth position, finger 1 plays the notes that fall on fret 5, finger 2 plays notes on the 6th fret, finger 3, the 7th, and finger 4 plays notes occurring on the 8th fret.

To play from this diagram, start on string 6 at fret 5 using finger 1 (index). Then, play string 6 at fret 8 with finger 4 (pinky).

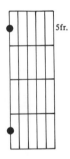

Next, play string 5 at fret 5 with finger 1, followed by fret 7 with finger 3 (ring).

Then, play string 4 at fret 5 with finger 1, followed by fret 7 with finger 3 (middle).

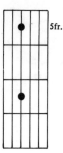

Next, play string 3 at fret 5 with finger 1, and then fret 7 with finger 3.

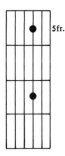

Then, play string 2 at fret 5 with finger 1, followed fret 8 with finger 4.

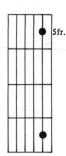

Finally, play string 1 at fret 5 with finger 1, and then fret 8 with finger 4.

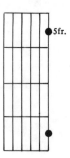

This completes the scale ascending. Reverse this sequence to play it descending. The complete scale (ascending and descending) appears on your tape as Ex. 9.

Technical Tips

Learn to play this scale (and all the others in this book) with alternate picking in your right hand. This means that you begin with a downstroke, play the next note with an upstroke, then another down, then another up, etc. Do not change this down-up-down-up sequence when you cross strings; each downstroke is always followed by an upstroke, each upstroke is always followed by a downstroke. This is the beginning of the kind of right-hand control that will let you play fast and clean.

Here is a diagram of the blues scale in A for Pattern 1. Pattern 1 in any key will be the one in which the root or keynote (in this case, A) is played on string 6 with finger 1.

Ex. 10 - 12

This pattern (ascending and descending) appears on your tape as Ex. 10. Notice that the only difference between this and the minor pentatonic scale we have already learned is one note, played in two places (string 5, fret 6 and string 3, fret 8). This note is called the *flatted-fifth* or *flat-five.* It is one of the bluesiest sounding notes of them all!

You need to have this pattern mastered before learning the next patterns. One good way to learn this scale and to get a feeling for its flavor is to practice it with your tape. Ex. 11 and 12 on your tape consist of a lead guitar on the right channel playing this pattern while the band (on the left) plays the first blues progression we learned in the last chapter. In Ex. 11, the guitar plays one note for each beat in a measure. In Ex. 12, the guitar plays three notes (a triplet) for each beat in a measure. This reinforces the shuffle rhythm of this progression.

Once you have both ways of playing this pattern under control, you can begin experimenting with the scale. Play Ex. 2 on your tape. While it is playing, try playing different notes from the pattern. It doesn't matter what order you play them in—jump around and try different things.

You will notice that every note sounds good no matter which chord is playing at the time, except for the flat-five which needs to move up or down to the next note in the scale. (This is called *resolution.*)This is why the blues is such a great place to begin improvising: Unlike many other forms of music, all the notes sound good all the time. This leaves you free to develop a sense of style, timing and phrasing of your own before going on to music of a more complex harmonic nature where the notes work differently against each chord, and you must know which notes to use with which chords.

This is also why we are able to learn blues scales as patterns, without having to know the names of the notes we are playing or their harmonic relationship to the chords they are working against. (That kind of knowledge is, of course, helpful to improving your blues and rock playing, and essential to playing any kind of jazz.)

Now that you have Pattern 1 under control, and some kind of feel for the way this music sounds, it is time to learn the rest of the patterns for the key of A, and how to connect them.

This is Pattern 0. (It is actually a low inversion of Pattern 5, but since it appears here below Pattern 1, we will refer to it as Pattern 0.) Notice that its notes are lower in pitch, that it is played at lower-numbered frets and that it uses only the two lowest strings. None of the patterns and extensions we will learn (except for Pattern 1) use all six strings. (There are full six-string patterns for each of these, but these smaller segments are the most used.)

Ex. 13

Practice playing Pattern 0 ascending and descending. This appears as Ex. 13 on your tape. Since there are only four notes in this pattern, you should be able to master it fairly quickly.

Now you need to learn how to connect Pattern 0 to Pattern 1.

Notice that Pattern 0 ends at string 5, fret 5. Notice also that this same note (string 5, fret 5) appears in Pattern 1 played with a different finger. What we need now is a way to get from one fingering to the other. There are actually two ways to do this.

First, let's connect the patterns with a *slide*. When you slide, you finger a note, pick it, and then leaving the full finger pressure on, move the finger to another fret on the same string. When you slide, you hear not only the picked note and the note you are sliding to, but also (briefly) the notes in between.

Here's Ex. 14 on your tape. This is Pattern 0 joined to Pattern 1 by a slide. Notice that in Pattern 0 you pick string 5, fret 5, finger 3 and slide smoothly to fret 7 (do not pick again).

Practice this until you can match the tape. Now, here's how to connect these patterns by a *shift*.

This is Ex. 15 on your tape. Notice that you do not hear the note in between string 5, fret 5 and string 5, fret 7. This technique is described below.

To shift, you must play the last note in the lower position (in this case, string 5, fret 5, finger 3) and then move very quickly to the next note in the higher position (string 5, fret 7, finger 3). While shifting, you let the other fingers of the left hand (in this case, fingers 1 and 2) rest lightly on the string to mute it until you reach the new position. In order to shift smoothly, you must stay on the last note in the lower position as long as possible, and then shift to the first note in the new position as quickly as possible.

This is Ex. 16 on your tape. Here, you are once again shifting from Pattern 0 to Pattern 1, but this time you are including the flat-five note at string 5, fret 6.

Play along with your tape and practice connecting these two patterns by shifting and by sliding. As you have done before, practice them one note per beat and three notes per beat. Once you have these connections mastered, you are ready to learn the next pattern, and how to connect it to the two patterns you already know.

This is Pattern 2, the next pattern above Pattern 1. It appears as Ex. 17 on your tape. Practice playing this pattern ascending and descending with the various rhythm styles on your tape. Once you have mastered it, you are ready to learn how it connects to Pattern 1.

Ex. 17

This is Ex.18 on your tape. In this example, you are connecting Pattern 1 to Patten 2 by a slide. When you reach string 3, fret 7, finger 3 in Pattern 1, put finger 2 where finger 3 is (switch fingers), and then pick and slide to fret 9.

Ex. 18

Be very precise when you practice this substitute-and-slide move— it's one you will use a lot! First, play string 3, fret 7, finger 3, then as one motion, put finger 2 where finger 3 was, pick the note and slide to fret 9. Finish out Pattern 2 from there.

Here is Ex .19 on your tape. This is one way of connecting Pattern 1 to Pattern 2 by a shift. Again, try to keep your shift very quick and clean.

Ex. 19

This is a diagram for the three patterns you have learned so far. Notice that they overlap in several places. At any of these spots, you can connect the patterns by a slide or by a shift. Just be sure you start and end with the correct fingers and connect the patterns smoothly. Try practicing these against your rhythm tracks until you can play one note per beat and three notes per beat steadily while making smooth pattern connections.

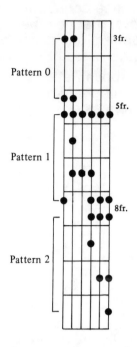

Below is a complete version of one way of connecting Pattern 0 to Pattern 1 and continuing through Pattern 2 by sliding, first ascending, and then descending. Notice that you are sliding past the flat-five notes and don't really hear them. This is Ex. 20 on your tape. Practice this until you have it very smooth and controlled.

Ex. 20

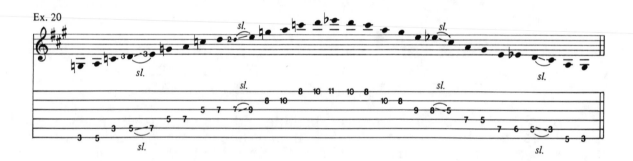

These are the same patterns, joined at the same connecting points as Ex. 20, but this time they are joined by shifts, and no notes are skipped. This is Ex. 21 on your tape. Again, master this before moving on.

Ex. 21

Now we'll learn the remaining four patterns. You can join them at any place they overlap with other patterns, and you can join them by a shift or by a slide. This is all still the blues scale in the key of A—that is, the same six notes in different octaves. You know from your own experiments that any of these notes sound good with any of the chords for the key of A (except for the flat-five sometimes), so experiment here also. Jump from one position to another, try things out, find things that sounds good to you.

It is important to begin experimenting early, and finding some sense of what you like. Otherwise, when you begin learning riffs from really great players, you may find yourself intimidated, and end up copying other players' styles instead of finding your own. Your goal in playing blues is always to express yourself. To that end, all players borrow from other sources, but they also invent their own phrasings, or alter what they borrow to make it their own. Even the small experiments you have done already are an important beginning toward finding your style.

This is Pattern 3. It appears (ascending and descending) on your tape as Ex. 22. Practice joining this pattern to Pattern 2 at all the overlap points you can find. Be careful to shift and slide smoothly, and to use the correct fingerings.

Ex. 22

Technical Tips

It is very important to get your pinky strong and independent—without it, you lose one-fourth of your fingers! Here is an excercise to help build up your pinky. Go to seventh position. Put finger 1 down on string1 at fret 7, and finger 2 down on string 1 at fret 8 (both at the same time). Leave these two fingers down for the whole excercise; do not move them at all. Then play this:

Play this as many times in a row as you can, and play it gradually faster and faster until you are playing just as fast as you can. At all times, play smoothly—with no breaks in sound between notes.

This is Pattern 4. It appears (ascending and descending) as Ex. 23 on your tape.

Ex. 23

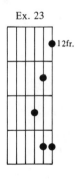

This is Pattern 5, ascending and descending. It appears as Ex. 24 on your tape.

Ex. 24

This is the Connector Pattern (ascending and descending, it appears as Ex. 25 on your tape). Be careful to get the shift in this pattern correct (you may slide or shift).

Ex. 25

All the patterns can be played an octave (12 frets) higher. How high you can go is limited only by the number of frets on your guitar. (Electric guitars vary in their number of frets—they usually have 21 to 24 frets.) Patterns above the 12th fret may be played an octave (12 frets) lower.

Once you have all these patterns under control, you'll be ready to learn how to use them. In Chapter III, we'll learn about riffs—what they are, how to invent them and how to use them. We'll look at examples of riffs used by some of the great players. Be sure you can play one note per beat and three notes per beat with your tape, and be able to move easily from pattern to pattern all over the neck before going on.

Michael Bloomfield

Chapter III.   Riffs and How To Use Them

Most blues and rock lead playing is built on riffs. In this chapter, we're going to learn what they are, some ways to construct them and some ways to use them.

The Basics

You need to know the blues scale in all the patterns taught in Chapter II.

Riffs are short musical statements or phrases. They are used (along with other devices) to organize a solo and give it some sense of coherence. You have practiced playing notes from the blues scale along with your tape. You have probably noticed that while all the notes sounded good with all the chords, just playing notes in no particular sequence gets pretty dull after a while. Learning different ways to use riffs is the first and most important technique to master to create interesting, coherent solos.

To get you started, I will show you one way to make a coherent solo using riffs. To play this solo, you first need to create and play three riffs that each meet three requirements. (These requirements are for this solo, they are not for all solos.)

Make up some riffs using these three rules:

1. Use only notes in the blues scale
2. Keep riffs four beats in length
3. Leave at least the last part of beat 4 silent

Here are examples of a few riffs that meet these requirements. These appear on your tape as Ex. 26. They are played against a click track so you can hear the timing of the notes in relation to the beats. Each one is played twice. Notice that because part of beat 4 has no activity, there is a pause before the riff is repeated.

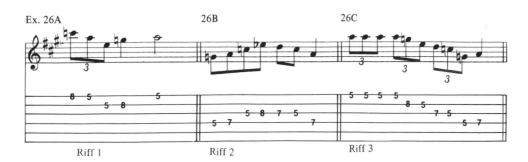

Ex. 26A   26B   26C

Riff 1   Riff 2   Riff 3

Ex. 27 is a riff with no silence in beat 4. Notice how hard it is to tell where the first time through the riff ends and the second time through begins. You can see that the pause between the riffs makes it easier to tell them apart.

Ex. 27

19

Invent five or six riffs of your own and learn to play them well. Be sure that they follow all three rules.

Once you have your riffs under control, you are ready to learn to use them. First, listen to Ex. 28 on your tape. This is the first riff from Ex. 26 being played against two different chords. In the first bar, it is being played against an A7 chord. In the second bar, it is being played against a D9 chord. The important thing to hear is that even though the lead guitar is playing the same exact riff in both bars, playing it against the two different chords makes it sound as if you are playing different riffs! This is a very useful thing to know, because one of the best and most commonly used devices for organizing a solo is repetition, and now you can begin to see how much variety this device can provide.

Ex. 28

Now, you are ready to learn a way to organize a solo using the riffs you have invented. This appears as Ex. 29 on your tape. In this example, I am using the three riffs from Ex. 26, and I am playing against the slow shuffle from Ex. 2.

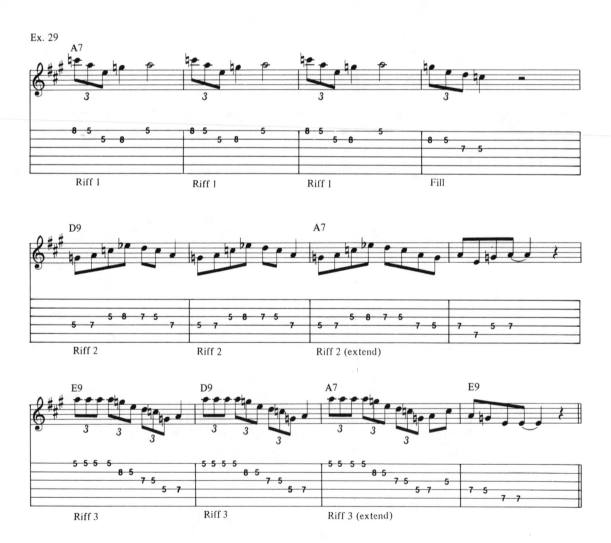

Above, you will see the chord progression written out, and underneath each bar is written what is being played in that bar. The first riff is played in bar 1, then repeated in bars 2 and 3. In bar 4, I am playing a fill (which I will explain below). In bars 5 and 6, the second riff is played, and in bar 8 the second riff is played and extended (again, the explanation follows). Finally, in bars 9 and 10, the third riff is played, and in bar 11, the third riff is played and extended.

A few things to notice:

Notice that all riff repeats are exact; that is, the timing of the notes is exactly the same, and the place in the bar where the riff starts is the same. Thus, the first riff starts on beat 2 each time, the second riff starts on beat 1 each time, etc.

Notice, also, that the pauses after phrases help the music breathe, making it easier to listen to, understand and enjoy.

Now, about fills and extensions. A *fill* is a short phrase just like a riff. The difference is that it is spontaneous—you invent it on the spot. Notice that in Ex. 29, there is a pause before and after the fill.

An *extension* is also a spontaneous phrase, but in an extension there is no pause beforehand, only afterwards. The extension is added on to the end of the riff it follows, making that riff seem longer (extending it).

Try playing a solo of this type against Ex. 2 on your tape using three of the riffs you have invented. Keep your fills and extensions short at first, and make sure you have all the pauses in the right places.

The next way to work with your short riffs is by using variations. Here is a riff with two variations. This appears as Ex. 30 on your tape. Notice that the differences between the riff and its variations are small.

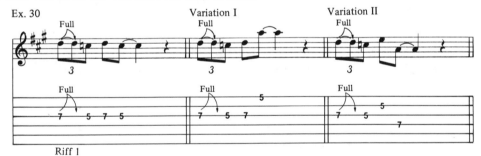

Technical Tips

The riff in Ex. 30 uses a technique called *string bending*. When you bend a string, you are raising the pitch of that string. You can bend up to a pitch the same as the note one fret higher, two frets higher, or more, limited only by your strength and how far your strings will bend before breaking. In the blues scale, you may bend any note up to the pitch of the next note in the scale. Here are the most common bends in Patterns 0,1 and 2.

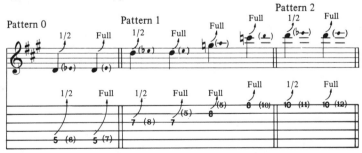

The arrows indicate which notes you can bend, and to which pitch they can be bent. Learn these, and then find as many other places as you can where you can easily bend a note up to the pitch of the next note in the scale.

Try making up a few riffs with variations of your own. Once you have those, you will be ready to learn some ways to use them.

Ex. 31 consists of two more riffs, each with two variations.

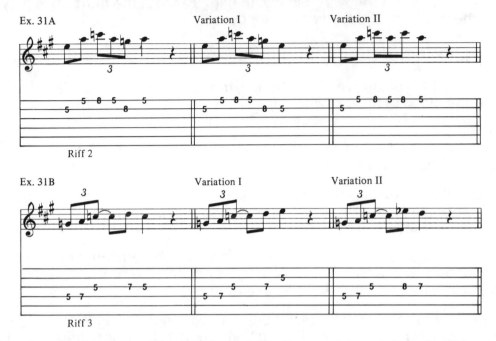

Now, play the riffs from Ex. 30 and 31, and the first variation of each. This appears on your tape as Ex. 32. Notice that the variations played are always variations of the riff preceding them. For example, in bar 1, you play Riff 1, and in bar 2, you play the first variation of Riff 1, etc.

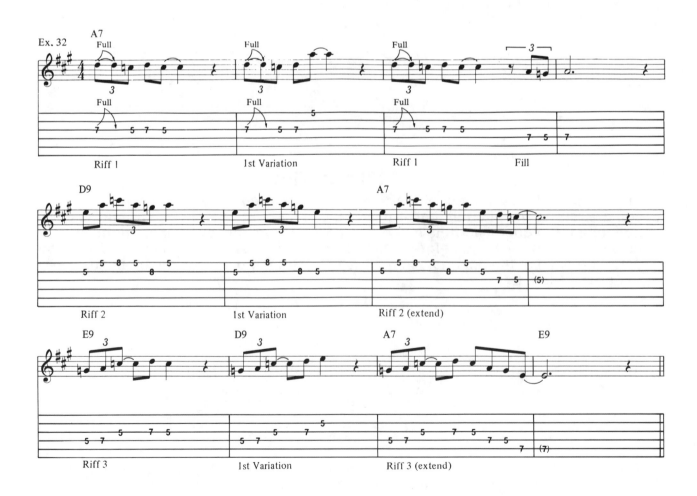

Or try this using the riffs and the two variations of each riff. This is Ex. 33:

Again, the variations marked in each line are variations of the riff used in the first bar of that line.

How interesting these solos are will depend on how interesting your licks, variations, fills and extensions are. Try inventing lots of different riffs, as well as learning riffs from recorded sources. When you listen to great players, notice that each player has his own style and sound. This is what your real goal is here: not just to copy, but to take original ideas and borrowed ideas and work them into a style that is distinctly your own.

Now, we'll learn some short riffs in the styles of several great players. These are all riffs that you could use in the type of riff-based solo we have learned so far. Many of them start near the end of a bar and end just after the beginning of the next bar. To use these, start before bar 1, and play all your repeats with the same timing.

For example, here is a riff that Eric Clapton has used. This is Ex. 34 on your tape.

Ex. 34

Technical Tips

This riff makes use of a device called a *slide.* A lot of the riffs you are going to learn use this technique as well as two other techniques: the *hammer-on* and the *pull-off.* You need to be able to execute all three.

Slides are executed three ways:

1) Here is a slide from an indeterminate point. You start a few frets below the note you are sliding to, pick and quickly slide to the note, keeping full pressure on the finger as you slide. This appears as Ex. 35 on your tape.

Ex. 35

2) Here is the same idea applied to the end of a note—play the note and then slide up or down to an arbitrary point. This is Ex. 36 on the tape.

Ex. 36

3) In this case, you play the first note and then slide to the second without picking again (Ex. 37). This is the same type of slide that you have already learned to use to connect blues scale patterns together.

Ex. 37

Now, let's look at two other important phrasing techniques, the hammer-on and the pull-off.

This is an example of the hammer-on. To perform it, you pick the first note and then slam your left-hand finger on the second note so that it sounds. Do not pick the second note. This is Ex. 38 on your tape.

Ex. 38

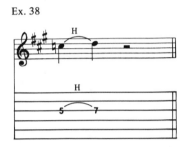

This is an example of a pull-off. You execute this by first putting the fingers for both notes on the fingerboard with pressure on (in this case, fingers 1 and 3). Next, pick the first note, and then without picking again, pull off with finger 3, causing the second note (finger 1) to sound (Ex. 39 on the tape).

Ex. 39

Finally, here are three examples of hammer-on/pull-off combinations. In the first example, you place both fingers on the fingerboard, pull off to the lower note, and then hammer on the third note (which is on a different string). This is often combined with a note bend. The second example shows this combination. The third example is a *trill*. In this example, you play the first note, hammer on the second, and pull off back to the first. This can be repeated indefinitely. All three of these appear as Ex. 40 on the tape.

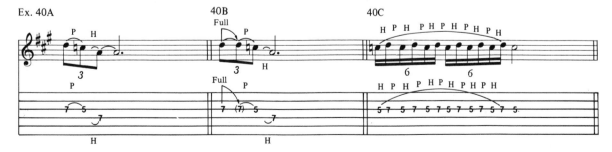

Here is how you would play the riff from Ex. 34 against the first line of the Ex. 2 rhythm track. Notice that there appear to be five bars on the line. The first bar is your count-off bar, and you start the first riff during the count-off. This is Ex. 41 on your tape. Notice that the fill is still in the same place as before.

Ex. 41

N.C.   A7   D9   A7

| / / / / ‖ / / / / | / / / / | / / / / | / / / / |

Riff 1   Riff 1   Riff 1   Fill 1

If you play with friends or in a band, you will probably play a progression like this several times, taking turns playing lead and rhythm. If your turn to play lead is not the first time through the progression, you would start this riff in the last bar of the preceding time through. The last bar is in the same time relationship to the first bar of the next repeat that the count-off bar is to the first bar of the progression, as shown. This is Ex. 42 on your tape.

Ex. 42

E9   D9   A7   D9   A7   E9

| / / / / | / / / / | / / / / | / / / / ‖

Riff 1--

A7

| / / / / | / / / / | / / / / | / / / / ‖

Riff 1   Riff 1   Riff 1

Moving right along:

Here are three more riffs in Eric Clapton's style. These appear as Ex. 43 through 45 on your tape.

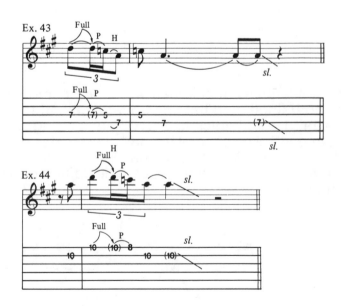

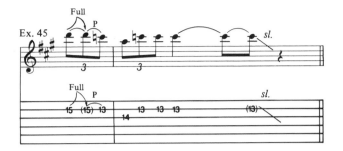

Mike Bloomfield used these three. These are Ex. 46 through 48.

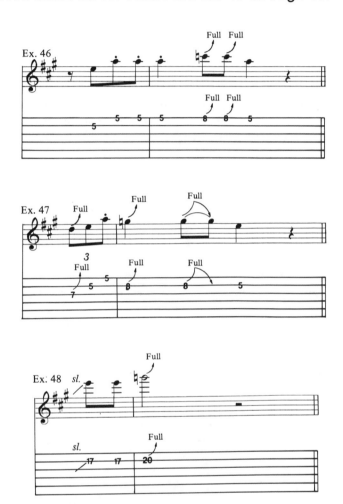

Here are three from B.B. King. These are Ex. 49 through 51.

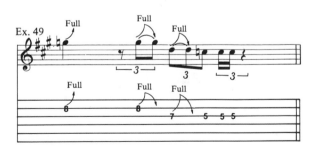

Ex. 50

Ex. 51

Jimmy Page uses all four of these. These appear as Ex. 52 through 55 on your tape. Notice how similar Ex. 55 is to Ex. 47 in Mike Bloomfield's style. The difference is mostly one of phrasing—exactly when and how long each note is played. Every blues player plays some form of this riff.

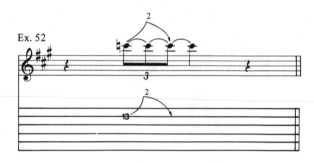

Ex. 52

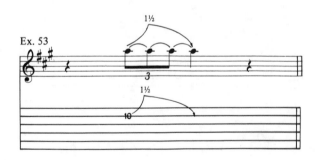

Ex. 53

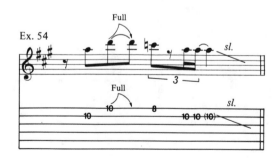

Ex. 54

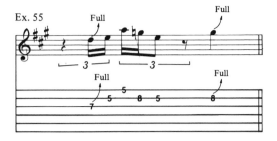

Here are two from Jimi Hendrix. These are Ex. 56 and 57.

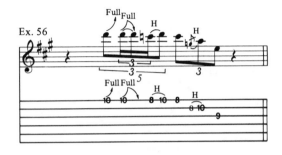

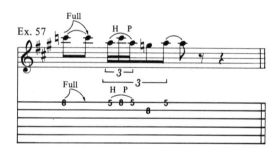

Alvin Lee of Ten Years After plays these two. These are Ex. 58 and 59.

Last, here's one each from Johnny Winter, Albert Collins, and Son Seals. These are Ex. 60 through 62.

Now that you have this first solo idea based on one-bar riffs under control, let's learn another way to organize a solo with riffs. This time, the riffs will be two bars in length, and we will use the rhythm track from Ex. 3 to work with.

Here are three riffs we will use in the next example. These were constructed using the same rules used to create your one-bar riffs, the only difference being that they are two bars in length, and the pause is left for part of beat 4 in the second bar only. These appear as Ex. 63 on your tape.

Ex. 63B

Ex. 63C

Now, here is the first way of using them. This is Ex. 64 on your tape.

Ex. 64

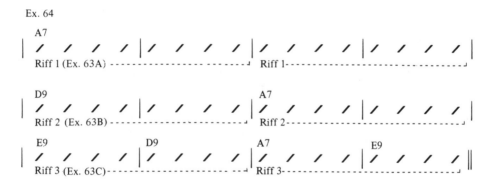

Notice that in this example, you don't need to use fills or extensions. You can, if you'd like, use variations of the riffs when you repeat them. First, here are variations for each of the riffs in Ex. 63. This is Ex. 65 on your tape.

Ex. 65A

Here is a solo using these variations. This is Ex. 66.

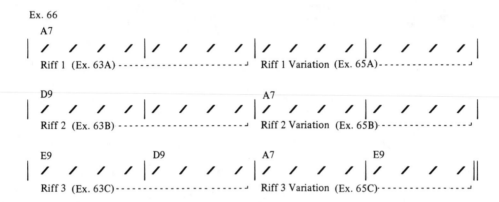

Here are several riffs that are two bars in length. You may use these in any of the solo types we have just learned.

These two are from Albert King. They appear as Ex. 67 and 68 on your tape.

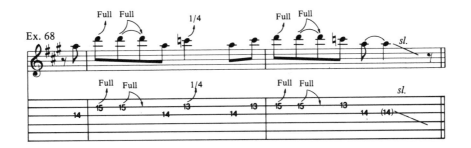

Johnny Winter plays both of these (Ex. 69 and 70).

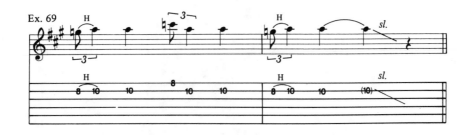

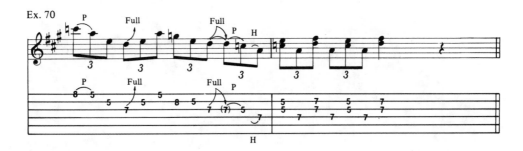

These two have a pronounced triplet feel. The first is from Elvin Bishop (Ex. 71), the second from Stevie Ray Vaughan (Ex. 72).

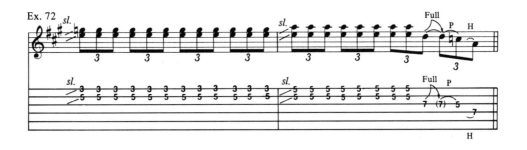

B. B. King

These two are from two great Chicago players. The first (Ex. 73) is from Lonnie Brooks, the second (Ex. 74) is from Albert Collins.

Eric Clapton has used all four of these. These are Ex. 75 through 78.

Here are two from Alvin Lee (Ex. 79 and 80). The first has been used by many players, the second is more characteristically Lee's.

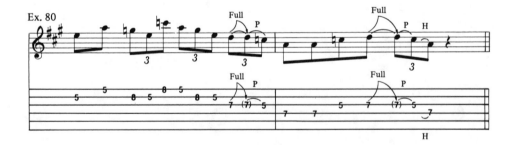

Dickie Betts plays the first one here (Ex. 81), and a great Chicago player named Donald Kinsey of The Kinsey Report plays the second (Ex. 82).

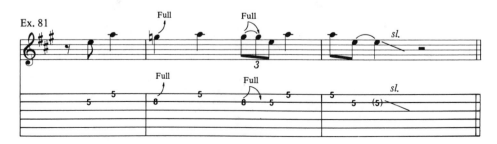

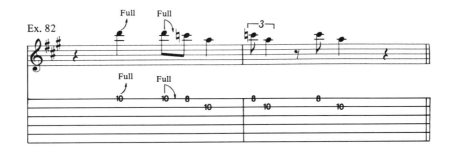

An exciting new guitarist named Jeff Healey plays both of these (Ex. 83 and 84).

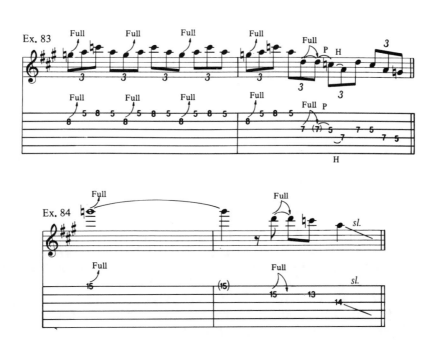

You can also play a solo using two-bar riffs by using six different riffs like this:

Ex. 85 on your tape is comprised of six riffs—the three riffs from Ex. 64, Ex. 79, Ex. 77 and Ex. 76.

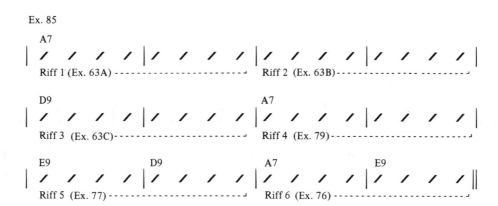

Up to this point, we have used only riffs that will work with any of the chords, and can be used interchangeably. The next type of solo we are going to learn uses a type of riff called a *turnaround*, and can be used in only one place in a progression.

Theory Notes

The V7 chord in any key (or its substitutions) serves the harmonic function of forcing (resolving) the chords back to the I (tonic) chord.

In the key of A, the V7 chord is E7 (we have been substituting E9), and the I chord is A (we have been playing A7). Play an A chord (not an A7). Notice that it sounds fine by itself, and when you play it, you don't feel any need to follow it with another chord. Now play E7 (not E9). Notice that when you play this chord, you immediately feel the need for another chord to follow it. The chord you need here is A. Play E7 followed by A. Notice how the E7 forces you to play the A to release the tension created by the E7.

Here are diagrams for an A chord and an E7 chord:

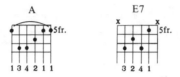

Chord progressions that end on the V7 chord (or its substitutions) and appear at the end of musical pieces are called *turnarounds* because they force you back to the beginning of the piece so that you may repeat it. In all of our blues progressions, the last bar has been a turnaround. You can play these blues pieces over and over again indefinitely, thanks to the turnaround. When you want to end the piece, simply play the I chord instead of the turnaround. Here is an example of a fast shuffle that ends instead of turning around. This is Ex. 86 on your tape.

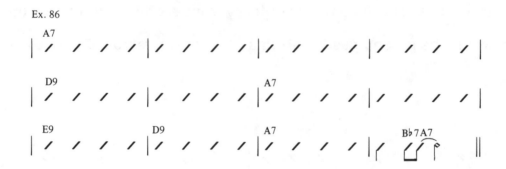

Listen to Ex. 87. It is very similar to the last type of solo that we learned. The difference is that in this solo the last riff is a turnaround riff (the first five riffs are the same as in Ex. 85). Turnaround riffs are like other riffs except that they emphasize the V7 chord at the end, usually by ending on one of the notes in the V7 chord. Here is the turnaround riff at the end of Ex. 87:

Now, we're going to learn turnaround riffs from some of the great players. Some of these use notes other than blues scale notes. We'll learn more about the how's and why's of this a little later.

The next two have been played by everybody. These are Ex. 88 and 89 on your tape. This is more easily played using the pick and the ring finger than with just the pick.

Here are two from Freddy King. These are Ex. 90 and 91. For Ex. 91 you will have to use the pick and ring finger combination.

These two are from Buddy Guy, one of the Chicago greats (Ex. 92 and 93).

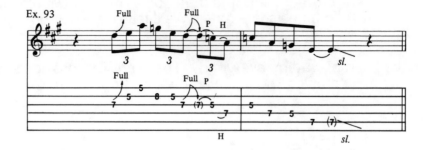

These two are from Son Seals. They appear as Ex. 94 and 95 on your tape.

Eric Clapton plays both of these (Ex. 96 and 97).

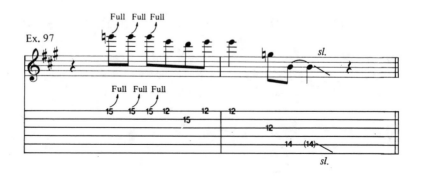

Here are two from Albert Collins (Ex. 98 and 99).

Alvin Lee plays the first one, Johnny Winter plays the second (Ex. 100 and 101).

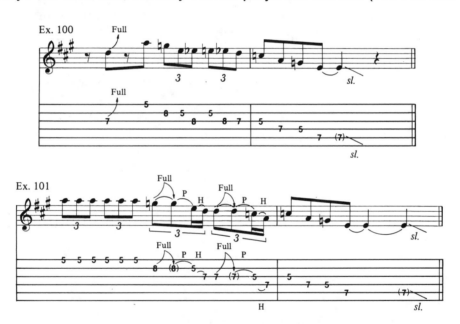

Some turnaround riffs are geared to a specific key because they use open strings for some of the notes in that key.

Here's one from Stevie Ray Vaughan that works only in the key of E. To use it, you must be playing in key of E. Notice how different this sounds from the other riffs. That's because of the distinctive open string sound (Ex. 102).

You can also play riffs that fill four bars. Here are two examples of four-bar riffs. These appear on your tape as Ex. 103.

Here's how you would use these in a blues. Notice that in the last line, you would play two two-bar riffs, one of which could be a turnaround. I am using the riffs from Ex. 80 and Ex. 93 for these two. This works best when played at a faster tempo (Ex. 104).

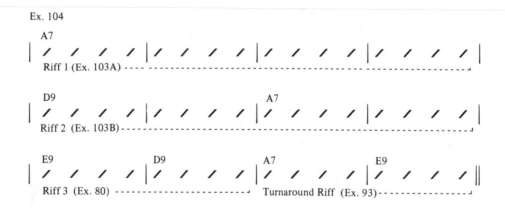

Here are some four-bar riffs from various players:

Let's start off with two from B.B. King. These are Ex. 105 and 106.

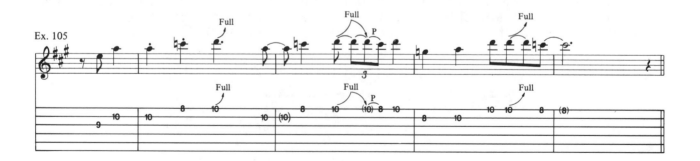

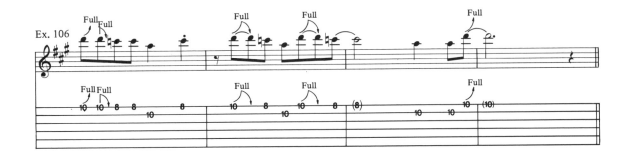

These three are from Donald Kinsey. They appear as Ex. 107 through 109 on your tape.

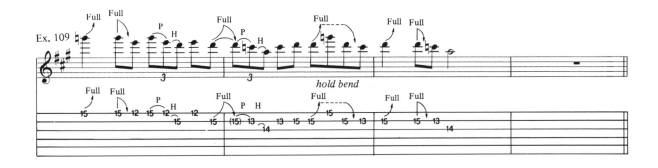

Eric Clapton plays these two (Ex. 110 and 111).

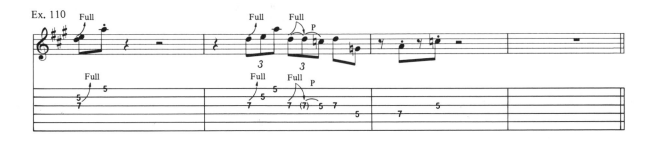

This one's from Lonnie Brooks (Ex. 112).

These two are from Alvin Lee (Ex. 113 and 114).

Here are two from Buddy Guy. These are Ex. 115 and 116.

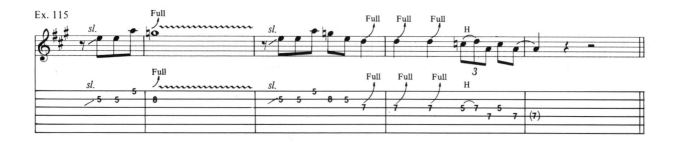

Elvin Bishop plays both of these (Ex. 117 and 118).

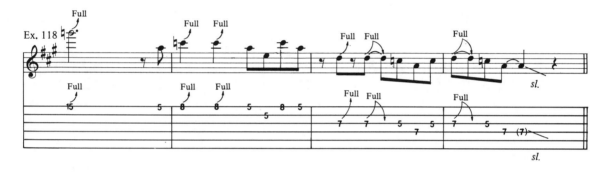

This one's from Son Seals. It appears on your tape as Ex. 119.

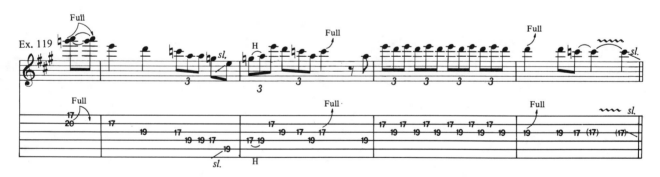

Freddy King Plays these two (Ex. 120 and 121).

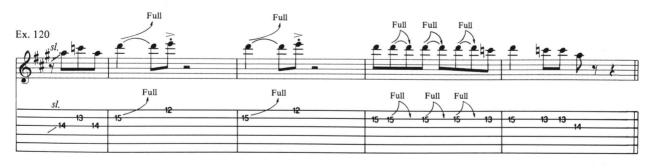

These two are from Albert Collins. They are Ex. 122 and 123.

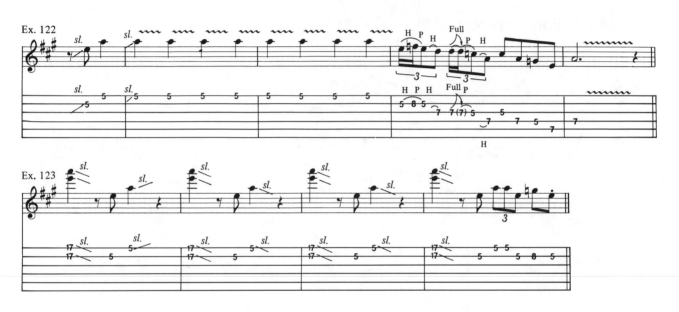

Finally, here's a tricky one from Johnny Winter. This one uses some out-of-scale notes. This is Ex. 124.

Up to this point, all of the chord progressions and riffs we have played have been in shuffle rhythms—rhythms where each beat is divided into three parts. In Volume II, we'll learn how to work with straight eighth-note patterns, explore a number of other methods for organizing solos, and learn how to make the blues have a major or minor feel.

Roy Buchanan

ABOUT THE AUTHOR

Michael Wolfsohn was born in Chicago in 1950. He began playing the piano at age eight, but soon discovered Pete Seeger and the guitar. During the 60's and 70's he developed an interest in rock, blues and many other styles of music, and learned to play several instruments. He has been playing, teaching and recording professionally since 1974, and has taught at Chicago's Old Town School of Folk Music and Northwestern University. He currently lives and teaches in New York City.